EXPLORING THE STATES

Oklahoma

THE SOONER STATE

by Blake Hoena

BLASTOFF! READERS
5

BELLWETHER MEDIA · MINNEAPOLIS, MN

Note to Librarians, Teachers, and Parents:

Blastoff! Readers are carefully developed by literacy experts and combine standards-based content with developmentally appropriate text.

Level 1 provides the most support through repetition of high-frequency words, light text, predictable sentence patterns, and strong visual support.

Level 2 offers early readers a bit more challenge through varied simple sentences, increased text load, and less repetition of high-frequency words.

Level 3 advances early-fluent readers toward fluency through increased text and concept load, less reliance on visuals, longer sentences, and more literary language.

Level 4 builds reading stamina by providing more text per page, increased use of punctuation, greater variation in sentence patterns, and increasingly challenging vocabulary.

Level 5 encourages children to move from "learning to read" to "reading to learn" by providing even more text, varied writing styles, and less familiar topics.

Whichever book is right for your reader, Blastoff! Readers are the perfect books to build confidence and encourage a love of reading that will last a lifetime!

This edition first published in 2014 by Bellwether Media, Inc.

No part of this publication may be reproduced in whole or in part without written permission of the publisher. For information regarding permission, write to Bellwether Media, Inc., Attention: Permissions Department, 5357 Penn Avenue South, Minneapolis, MN 55419.

Library of Congress Cataloging-in-Publication Data

Hoena, B. A.
  Oklahoma / by Blake Hoena.
    p. cm. – (Blastoff! readers. Exploring the states)
  Includes bibliographical references and index.
  Summary: "Developed by literacy experts for students in grades three through seven, this book introduces young readers to the geography and culture of Oklahoma"–Provided by publisher.
  ISBN 978-1-62617-035-3 (hardcover : alk. paper)
  1. Oklahoma–Juvenile literature. I. Title.
  F694.3.H64 2014
  976.6–dc23
                                                                    2013009359

Printed in the United States of America, North Mankato, MN.

Table of **Contents**

Where Is Oklahoma?

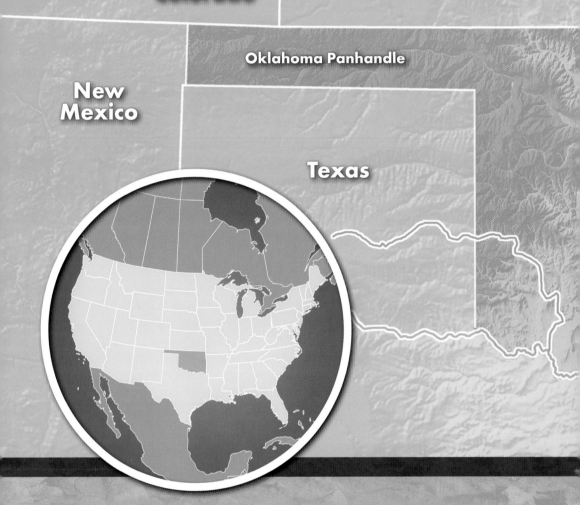

Colorado

Oklahoma Panhandle

New Mexico

Texas

Oklahoma is located in the south-central United States. Texas lies to the south. The Red River forms much of the border between the two states. Missouri and Arkansas lie east of Oklahoma. Kansas and Colorado are to the north. A thin strip of Oklahoma reaches west to New Mexico.

Kansas

Missouri

Tulsa

Broken Arrow

Oklahoma

★ Oklahoma City

• Norman

Arkansas

N

W · E

S

Red River

Oklahoma lies halfway between the east and west coasts of the United States. This makes it an important center for transportation. In the center of the state is Oklahoma City, the capital and largest city.

Native Americans once relied on Oklahoma's large herds of bison for food and clothing. The first Europeans arrived in the region in 1541. Later, the United States gained the land in the **Louisiana Purchase**. Throughout the 1800s, much of the area was known as Indian Territory. Oklahoma became the forty-sixth state in 1907.

Did you know?

The Oklahoma land rush was to begin at noon on April 22, 1889. Some people snuck into the area to claim land sooner than the law allowed. These settlers earned the state its nickname of the "Sooner State."

Oklahoma Timeline!

1541:	Francisco Vásquez de Coronado is the first European to explore Oklahoma.
1803:	The United States buys land that includes Oklahoma in the Louisiana Purchase.
1830s:	Thousands of Native Americans are forced to move west. They are sent to Indian Territory in Oklahoma.
1889:	The Oklahoma land rush begins. The U.S. government allows white settlers to claim land in parts of Oklahoma.
1907:	Oklahoma becomes the forty-sixth state.
1930s:	A lack of water causes land to dry out and crops to fail. Thousands of Oklahomans move west to find better conditions.
1995:	A terrorist bombs the Alfred P. Murrah Federal Building in Oklahoma City.
2013:	A massive tornado kills more than 20 people and destroys hundreds of homes in Moore.

Oklahoma City bombing

Francisco Vásquez de Coronado

Moore tornado destruction

The Land

Oklahoma can be broken up into several different regions. The Red River runs along the border with Texas. This is a region of swamps and **fertile** farmland. Just north of the river, several small mountain ranges rise above the land.

Along the state's eastern border is an area of steep river valleys. This is called the Ozark **Plateau**. From there the land slopes down into the Prairie **Plains**. In the middle of the state are wooded, rolling hills and dry grasslands. The land rises up into the Gypsum Hills and the High Plains along Oklahoma's western border. These are the driest regions of the state.

fun fact !

Oklahoma has 200 artificial lakes. That's more than any other state!

...region called Tornado Alley. The state averages around 55 tornadoes per year.

Oklahoma's Climate

average °F

spring
Low: 49°
High: 71°

summer
Low: 70°
High: 92°

fall
Low: 51°
High: 73°

winter
Low: 32°
High: 53°

The Oklahoma **Panhandle** stretches west along the top of Texas. This narrow strip of land is the highest part of Oklahoma. Much of the state's wheat is grown in the region. The area's grasslands are also perfect for raising cattle.

From 1850 to 1890, the Oklahoma Panhandle was unclaimed territory. Mostly cattlemen and their herds crossed through the empty land. Settlers arrived in the 1880s, but they could not officially own land. Many people called the region "No Man's Land." With no government to enforce rules, settlers took the law into their own hands. Today, the Oklahoma Panhandle is still associated with the Wild West.

Black Mesa

! fun fact

The highest point in Oklahoma is in the northwest corner of the Panhandle. Black Mesa rises 4,973 feet (1,516 meters) above sea level.

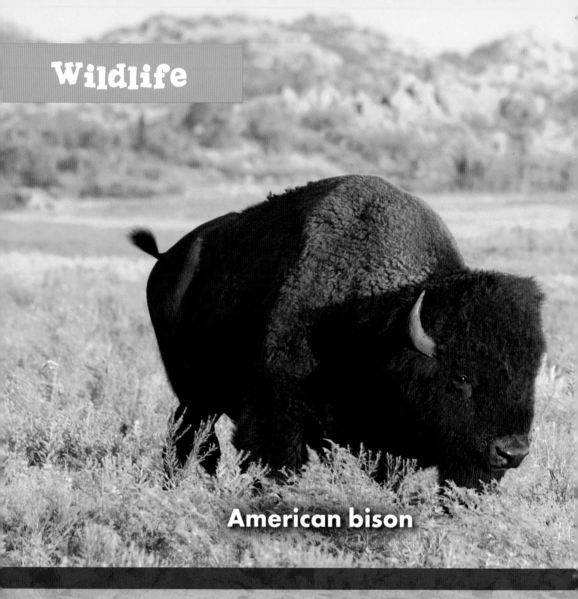

American bison

Prairies and grasslands stretch across Oklahoma. Buffalo grass and Indian grass cover large areas of the state. Wildflowers range from black-eyed Susans to verbena. Cactuses and sagebrush grow in the drier western regions. The eastern part of the state has thick forests. Oak, redbud, and sweet gum trees grow there.

roadrunner

Mexican free-tailed bat

armadillo

Armadillos, rattlesnakes, and other desert animals thrive in Oklahoma. White-tailed deer and American bison share the land with opossums, prairie dogs, and coyotes. The state's many birds include the roadrunner and the red-cockaded woodpecker.

Landmarks

Oklahoma has some amazing natural landmarks. The Gloss Mountains in the west are nicknamed the "Glass Mountains." Selenite crystals make the area's **mesas** and **buttes** sparkle like glass in the sunlight. The Wichita Mountains **Wildlife Refuge** is in southwestern Oklahoma. This protected area helped save bison from **extinction**. Today, it is home to many other **endangered** animals.

Other Oklahoma landmarks are human-made. A 1995 **terrorist** attack in Oklahoma City destroyed the Alfred P. Murrah Federal Building. The Oklahoma City National Memorial and Museum now resides where the building once stood. It honors the 168 people who died in the bombing, as well as those who survived.

Wichita Mountains Wildlife Refuge

Gloss Mountains

Oklahoma City
National Memorial and Museum

Tulsa is Oklahoma's second largest city. It stands along the Arkansas River in the northeast. The city's roots trace back to Native Americans. The Creek people were forced out of Alabama in the 1830s. They started a settlement in what is now Tulsa. Railroad tracks provided passage to the area in the early 1880s. This brought European settlers to Tulsa.

Did you know?
The first Creek settlers in Tulsa gathered under a large burr oak tree for ceremonies and feasts. The Creek Council Oak Tree still stands. It is now the central feature of a city park.

In 1901, oil was discovered in the area. Tulsa quickly changed from a small **pioneer** town to a **boomtown**. Thousands of people moved to the region looking for work. Hotels and businesses sprung up overnight. Today, Tulsa is home to many oil companies. It is also Oklahoma's most important **port city**.

Working

Did you know?
The Oklahoma National Stock Yards was founded in 1910 in Oklahoma City. It is the nation's largest cattle market. Thousands of cows and bulls are sold there weekly.

Mining plays a big role in Oklahoma. The state is a leading producer of oil and natural gas. Most of the oil wells are in the center of the state. Natural gas deposits are found all over. Coal, sand, and gravel are other mined products.

Farming and **manufacturing** are also important to Oklahoma. Ranchers raise cattle and horses. The state is also a leading producer of wheat. Factory workers help make machinery and transportation equipment. In bigger cities, Oklahomans have **service jobs** at banks, hotels, restaurants, and other places.

Where People Work in Oklahoma

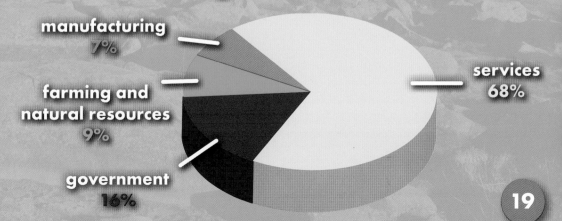

manufacturing
7%

farming and
natural resources
9%

government
16%

services
68%

Oklahoma has its roots in the Wild West. Cowboys used to drive large herds of cattle across its high plains and rolling grasslands. Today, horseback riding and **rodeos** are popular activities in the state. Oklahomans also enjoy fishing for trout and bass in the state's lakes and rivers. Oklahoma has 35 state parks for people who enjoy hiking, biking, and camping.

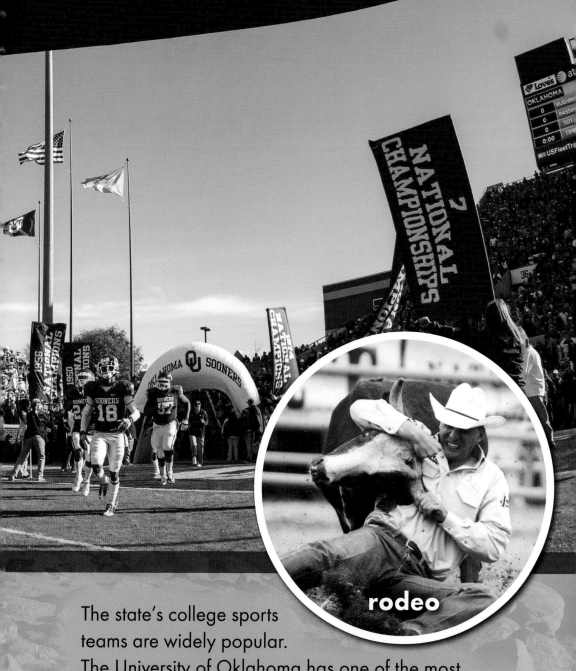

rodeo

The state's college sports teams are widely popular. The University of Oklahoma has one of the most successful football teams in the nation. Basketball and wrestling fans follow the Oklahoma State Cowboys. Oklahomans also appreciate the arts at museums, theaters, and orchestra concerts.

Chicken Fried Steak

Ingredients:

4 6-ounce rib eye steaks, about 1/2 inch thick

3/4 cup milk

1 egg

1 1/2 cups flour

1 teaspoon seasoned salt

1/2 teaspoon black pepper

Oil

Directions:

1. Trim fat off the steaks. Using a meat mallet or rolling pin, pound steaks to 1/4 inch thick.

2. Beat milk and egg in a shallow dish. Mix flour, salt, and pepper in another shallow dish. Set both dishes aside.

3. Add about 1/2 inch oil to a large skillet. Heat over medium-high heat.

4. Coat steaks in the egg and flour. Add to the pan. Cook until the bottom is browned, about 2 to 3 minutes.

5. Flip steaks and cook another 2 to 3 minutes. Do not overcook.

6. Place finished steaks on a paper towel-lined baking sheet. Keep warm until all steaks are cooked. Top with creamy gravy.

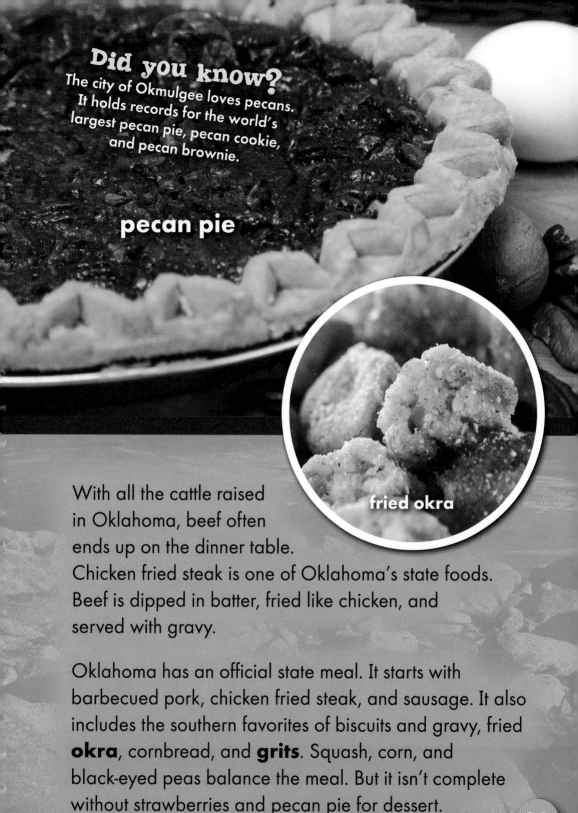

pecan pie

fried okra

With all the cattle raised in Oklahoma, beef often ends up on the dinner table. Chicken fried steak is one of Oklahoma's state foods. Beef is dipped in batter, fried like chicken, and served with gravy.

Oklahoma has an official state meal. It starts with barbecued pork, chicken fried steak, and sausage. It also includes the southern favorites of biscuits and gravy, fried **okra**, cornbread, and **grits**. Squash, corn, and black-eyed peas balance the meal. But it isn't complete without strawberries and pecan pie for dessert.

23

Festivals

Many festivals in Oklahoma highlight its Wild West and Native American roots. At the International Finals Youth Rodeo, young cowboys and cowgirls compete in barrel racing and steer wrestling contests. **Venomous** snakes take the spotlight at the Okeene Rattlesnake Roundup. Visitors can join a snake hunt and watch snake handlers in action.

Native Americans hold many festivals to honor their heritage. The Red Earth Native American Cultural Festival is held in Oklahoma City. Smaller **powwows** take place throughout the state. Native Americans display their art, perform dances, and celebrate their unique **traditions**.

Red Earth Native American Cultural Festival

International Finals
Youth Rodeo

Trail of Tears

In 1829, settlers discovered gold on Cherokee land in Georgia. Soon after, the U.S. government passed the Indian Removal Act. In 1838, thousands of Cherokee were forced from their land. They traveled through Tennessee, Kentucky, Illinois, Missouri, and Arkansas. They ended up in what is now Oklahoma. At the time, the area was set aside as Indian Territory.

Many of the Cherokee people traveled the nearly 1,000 miles (1,609 kilometers) on foot. Hundreds died on the trail. That is why the journey is called the "Trail of Tears." Museums and historic sites are now found along the route. Grounded in Native American culture and a Wild West past, Oklahoma honors its roots. Its heritage continues to be an important part of the state today.

Fast Facts About Oklahoma

Oklahoma's Flag

Oklahoma's state flag has a light blue background. It features an Osage shield decorated with eagle feathers. Two symbols of peace lay across the shield. One is a calumet, or peace pipe, and the other is an olive branch.

State Flower
Oklahoma rose

State Nicknames:	The Sooner State Boomer's Paradise
State Motto:	*Labor Omnia Vincit*; "Labor Conquers All Things"
Year of Statehood:	1907
Capital City:	Oklahoma City
Other Major Cities:	Tulsa, Norman, Broken Arrow
Population:	3,751,351 (2010)
Area:	69,899 square miles (181,038 square kilometers); Oklahoma is the 20th largest state.
Major Industries:	mining, farming, manufacturing
Natural Resources:	oil, natural gas, coal, soil, water
State Government:	101 representatives; 48 senators
Federal Government:	5 representatives; 2 senators
Electoral Votes:	7

State Animal
American bison

State Bird
scissor-tailed flycatcher

29

Glossary

boomtown—a town that experiences quick growth, usually because of the discovery of a natural resource such as gold or oil

buttes—small hills or mountains with steep sides and flat tops

endangered—at risk of becoming extinct

extinction—disappearing completely

fertile—able to support growth

grits—a porridge-like dish made of ground corn

Louisiana Purchase—a deal made between France and the United States; it gave the United States 828,000 square miles (2,144,510 square kilometers) of land west of the Mississippi River.

manufacturing—a field of work in which people use machines to make products

mesas—wide hills with steep sides and flat tops

native—originally from a specific place

okra—a green vegetable with a slippery texture

panhandle—a narrow part of a state that extends from the main area

pioneer—one of the first people to explore or settle an area

plains—large areas of flat land

plateau—an area of flat, raised land

port city—a city with one or more harbors where ships can dock

powwows—celebrations of Native American culture that often include singing and dancing

rodeos—events where people compete at tasks such as bull riding and calf roping; cowboys once completed these tasks as part of their daily work.

service jobs—jobs that perform tasks for people or businesses

terrorist—a person who performs a violent act to create fear among people

traditions—customs, ideas, or beliefs handed down from one generation to the next

venomous—producing a poisonous substance called venom

wildlife refuge—a natural area in which wildlife is protected

To Learn More

AT THE LIBRARY

Fradin, Dennis Brindell. *The Louisiana Purchase*. Tarrytown, N.Y.: Marshall Cavendish Benchmark, 2010.

Hesse, Karen. *Out of the Dust*. New York, N.Y.: Scholastic Press, 1997.

Strudwick, Leslie. *Oklahoma: The Sooner State*. New York, N.Y.: Weigl, 2012.

ON THE WEB

Learning more about Oklahoma is as easy as 1, 2, 3.

1. Go to www.factsurfer.com.

2. Enter "Oklahoma" into the search box.

3. Click the "Surf" button and you will see a list of related Web sites.

With factsurfer.com, finding more information is just a click away.

Index

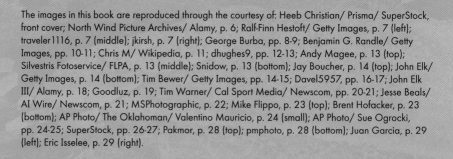

The images in this book are reproduced through the courtesy of: Heeb Christian/ Prisma/ SuperStock, front cover; North Wind Picture Archives/ Alamy, p. 6; Ralf-Finn Hestoft/ Getty Images, p. 7 (left); traveler1116, p. 7 (middle); jkirsh, p. 7 (right); George Burba, pp. 8-9; Benjamin G. Randle/ Getty Images, pp. 10-11; Chris M/ Wikipedia, p. 11; dhughes9, pp. 12-13; Andy Magee, p. 13 (top); Silvestris Fotoservice/ FLPA, p. 13 (middle); Snidow, p. 13 (bottom); Jay Boucher, p. 14 (top); John Elk/ Getty Images, p. 14 (bottom); Tim Bewer/ Getty Images, pp. 14-15; Davel5957, pp. 16-17; John Elk III/ Alamy, p. 18; Goodluz, p. 19; Tim Warner/ Cal Sport Media/ Newscom, pp. 20-21; Jesse Beals/ AI Wire/ Newscom, p. 21; MSPhotographic, p. 22; Mike Flippo, p. 23 (top); Brent Hofacker, p. 23 (bottom); AP Photo/ The Oklahoman/ Valentino Mauricio, p. 24 (small); AP Photo/ Sue Ogrocki, pp. 24-25; SuperStock, pp. 26-27; Pakmor, p. 28 (top); pmphoto, p. 28 (bottom); Juan Garcia, p. 29 (left); Eric Isselee, p. 29 (right).